D0848648

Saint Francis of Assisi

God's gentle knight

Pauline
BOOKS & MEDIA
BOSTON

Written by Françoise Vintrou

Illustrations by Augusta Curelli

Translation from the original French by Caroline Morson

Edited and adapted by Patricia Edward Jablonski, F.S.P.

© 1998, Éditions du Signe, 1 rue Alfred Kastler, B.P. 94 - 67038 Strasbourg

Printed in Spain by Beta Editorial

This is the wonderful story of St. Francis of Assisi. Before beginning to read it, turn to the back of this book. There you will find an explanation of some words that may be new to you.

Francis lived at a time when there were many knights. It was an exciting and adventurous time. And Francis loved adventure! In fact, he dreamed of being a knight.

Francis came from a wealthy family. He had a very nice house and lots of expensive clothes. But it wasn't enought to make him happy. Instead of wishing to be rich and powerful, Francis wanted to be poor and humble like Jesus. He wanted to serve others out of love as Jesus did. And so he did become a special kind of knight - a knight of God!

In the year 1182...
the beautiful little Italian town of Assisi stretched
out under the golden sun, nestled among the hills,
grapevines and silvery olive trees.

This is where a baby boy was born in September 1182. His father Peter Bernardone was in France at the time, and his mother Lady Pica named the baby John. When Mr. Bernardone returned home, he was so excited about his visit to France that he changed his son's name.

"We'll call him Francis," he said.

"*Peace and joy!*" a crier announced in the streets of Assisi. "The Bernardones have a new son!"

Mr. Bernardone was a cloth merchant who often traveled as part of his business. He was a rich man who knew how to make good deals. He already imagined Francis behind the counter of his store selling fine fabrics to wealthy customers.

Francis was born in the time of the knights, the crusades and the troubadours, who wrote poems and put them to music. It was the time when the great cathedrals were being built. In those days French was the language which all important and rich people spoke.

Lady Pica, Francis's mother, was a gentle woman. She loved little Francis so much and she took very good care of him. She would gently hum him songs to put him to sleep. Some of these were probably the beautiful songs sung by the troubadours.

Francis grew up in his happy family. He knew what it was like to be rich and to have everything he wanted. But there were many poor people without food in Italy at that time. Francis was loving and kind to the poor. Each time a beggar held out his hand, Francis had something to give.

Like other children his age, Francis went to school. His parents sent him to the school of St. George near the town walls. Francis was fascinated by the story his teacher told about how St. George killed the dragon.

In the winter Francis liked to sit in front of the big fireplace and watch the dancing flames. Was he dreaming that he was a warrior battling a dragon or rescuing a beautiful princess? Francis didn't have a suit of armor, but he had a brave heart. He wanted to become a knight. But how could he ever become a knight when his father was a cloth merchant?

It didn't matter. Just the thought of it made him happy. And he sang as he always did when he was happy.

Francis worked in the family store under his father's watchful eye.

"Look at these colors! Feel how fine this cloth is," he urged the customers who were charmed by his smile.

Mr. Bernardone was delighted to see his son becoming such a good salesman.

"He's a born merchant," he happily thought to himself.

Francis's joy in life began to dazzle people. He wanted to be first everywhere and people followed him. In his friendly way he knew how to get others to obey him. He was rich and elegant. Rumors spread about this merchant's son who behaved like a lord. When the neighbors repeated the rumors to Lady Pica, she gently replied, «Francis is a son of God.»

Francis turned fifteen. According to the custom in those days, he was now considered a man. He was always with the young nobles of the town.

Like them, Francis dressed in colorful woolen cloth, precious silk and fine velvet. He had many friends and he sang like a troubadour. Francis and his friends were a noisy group. They sang, danced, ate, drank and laughed late into the night, celebrating in the square and in the streets... and waking up the townspeople too! Francis and his friends loved to have fun.

"Come on and dance! One, two, three, tap your heels!"

Francis danced and sang in French to the happy beat of the tambourine.
His clear, strong voice echoed in the silence of the night. Even the stars seemed to be listening.

Peace and joy!

But not everyone was in the mood to celebrate. In those days there were many small wars going on between rival towns. Francis decided to join the army to defend Assisi against the town of Perugia. The battle was tough.

Francis was captured and kept as a prisoner for almost a year. He got very ill. His father managed to get him out of prison by paying a ransom.

Francis got better once he was home again. He tried to get a little exercise by walking around, but he still had to lean on a stick. One day he was finally able to go outside. It was a beautiful day. Francis could smell the cypress trees and hear the breeze rustling through the olive groves. But something was different. He didn't know why, but the cheerful countryside no longer made him feel happy.

19

Francis realized that his time in prison had changed him. What was happening? He wasn't sure. Soon he started dreaming about being a knight again. Then he decided to accompany a young lord on a mission to defend the pope. His father got him the best equipment, including armor, a horse, lance and shield. But on the way Francis met a knight who had lost everything in the war. Francis held out his gold-embroidered cloak and his weapons to him. "Take these. They're for you," he said.

Francis continued on his way. He stopped in the town of Spoleto the next night. There, while he was sleeping, he had a dream. A gentle voice called him and asked, "Francis, whom is it better to serve, the servant or the master?"

"The master," Francis whispered. "Lord, what do you want me to do?"

The voice answered, "Go back to the land where you were born and you will be told what to do."

Francis sold his armor and went back to Assisi. His father was upset that he had wasted so much money on the military equipment. He ordered Francis to return to work in the store. Only Lady Pica was happy about the change in Francis.

"My child will be a child of God," she said to herself.

Francis wasn't sure what to do with his life. But he felt that God was working powerfully in his heart. His friends didn't understand what was happening.

"You've forgotten us," they complained.

"What's up? You're so different now."

"I'm in love with God," Francis tried to explain.

Francis had never been so happy ! The world around him no longer seemed to exist. At home he stayed in his room where he prayed and praised God. Francis still sang... but differently !

Peace and joy !

Francis loved to walk alone in the countryside. One day he climbed up Mount Subiaso, far away from the noise of the town. Under the fir trees there he found a cave. He went inside.

There he wept for the times when he had not paid enough attention to God. His tears brought peace to his heart. He came out into the sunshine feeling light and joyful.

Francis kept trying to understand what God wanted him to do. One day, as he was out walking again, he came across the little church of San Damiano. It was very old and was falling apart. The walls had been worn away by the sun, the rain and time. Francis went inside.

A big crucifix caught his attention. He knelt down. "Lord, what do you want me to do?" he prayed. "Go, Francis, and rebuild my house," he heard God answer in his heart.

Francis thought God meant the church of San Damiano. But later on he realized that God wanted him to help rebuild the whole Catholic Church, which was very divided and troubled at that time.

Another day, as he was riding his horse, Francis heard the sound of the rattle which warned that a leper was passing by. Back then there was no cure for leprosy. People were very afraid of this disease and so anyone who caught it was driven out of town.

Instead of galloping away as he usually did when a leper came close, Francis got off his horse. He walked up to the leper and kissed him. Then his heart was filled with great joy and he began to sing.

Peace and joy!

His family couldn't understand what was going on.
Francis spent his time shut in his room praying. He
only came out to visit his new friends, the poor. What
had happened to the young man who loved parties?
Why had he given up his expensive clothes?

"Francis is really acting strange," muttered his brother
Angelo.

"As long as he's good at selling cloth in the store, it
doesn't bother me," his father answered.

One day, on his return from a trip, Mr. Bernardone asked, "Where has Francis disappeared to?"

"He's gone crazy!" his brother shouted. "He's sold his horse and some cloth from the store, too. He says he needs money to rebuild a church."

His father was furious. "He'll ruin me!" he cried. "I have to find him."

On April 12, 1206, Francis and his father had a big argument. Francis had started rebuilding and repairing the church of San Damiano. His father had tried to stop him.

"Francis, that's enough! Give me back my money and come home!"

"No, Father, my place is here. From now on, I'm only going to serve God."

"You refuse to obey me?" Mr. Bernardone roared. "We're going to the bishop about this!"

"Francis, you've really upset your father," said the bishop. "Give him back the money if you want to serve God. Have trust. The Lord will take care of you."
"You're right, Your Excellency. I don't want to owe my father anything," replied Francis as he took off his expensive clothes. "From now on I can truly say, 'Our Father, who art in heaven.'"
The crowd that had gathered to watch was very moved.

Francis stood there naked, just as he had been on the day he was born. The bishop covered him with his own cloak. In a mysterious way this day was like a new birth for Francis.

Dressed in rags, Francis left Assisi. He went to live in the forest where he sang with joy. Peace filled his heart. How good it was to breathe the pure air, see the clear sky and hear the beautiful song of the birds !

During the following years, Francis repaired San Damiano and many other ruined churches. He lived very poorly, begging for his food. All those who knew him made fun of him as walked through the streets of Assisi.

One day, on February 24, 1209, Francis heard the priest read the Gospel during Mass.

Jesus said, "Go out and proclaim everywhere that the Kingdom of Heaven is at hand. Take no gold nor silver, no traveling bag for the journey, no spare tunic or shoes or staff..."

"That's exactly what I want to do!" exclaimed Francis. He left behind his staff, his sandals, his cloak and belt. From then on he would be a disciple of Jesus, poor and free. He would be a knight of God!

Francis went out to preach the peace and joy of Jesus' Good News to everyone he met. The words just bubbled up in his heart which was overflowing with love. People listened in amazement. They no longer threw stones at him. They no longer called him crazy. Francis used simple, everyday words that everybody could understand. He preached in the streets and on the roads.

Everywhere he went
he called for peace and
forgiveness. He always
began his sermons by saying,
"May the Lord Jesus give you
peace!"

Peace and joy!

Francis's enthusiasm and faith made others want to follow him.

"Do you recognize me, Francis? It's me, Bernard de Quintevalle."

"Oh, Bernard, I'm so happy to see you again! I still remember the fun we had together..."

"I've admired you for a long time, Francis. Now I've decided to give up the world in order to share your life and follow in the footsteps of Jesus," Bernard eagerly explained.

"Give all that you own to the poor and come with me," Francis invited with a smile.

Little by little others joined them : Peter de Catane, Father Sylvester, Brother Giles, Brother Elijah, Brother Leo....

Day by day Francis began to understand that Jesus came into our world in order to serve and that he gave his life out of love for all people. He was moved to think that Jesus, who is God, washed the feet of his disciples. And so Francis wanted the men who shared his love of Jesus to be called "Friars Minor," which meant the brothers and loving servants of all.

In 1209, Francis and eleven of his brothers went to Rome. There Francis explained the Rule of his order to Pope Innocent III. The Pope approved it. The Franciscan family was born.

Francis sent his followers out two by two to preach peace and the Good News of the Gospel on the roads and in the villages. They visited Italy, France, Germany, Spain and even Egypt. As soon as they came across a crucifix or a church on the roadside, the brothers knelt down and recited the prayer that Francis had taught them:

"Lord Jesus, we adore you here and in the churches which are all over the earth, and we bless you because you have redeemed the world through your holy cross."

At that time a beautiful sixteen-year-old young woman was living in Assisi. Her name was Clare Offreduccio. She belonged to a noble family. One day, after she heard Francis preach, Clare went to find him.

"Like you, I want to follow Jesus who is poor," she said, "I want to give my life to God."

Since her family didn't agree with her decision, Clare had to run away from home. On the night of March 18, 1212, she escaped through a back door while everyone was sleeping. She ran down the slopes of the hill to join Francis and the brothers. In front of the altar of the little chapel of St. Mary of the Angels, Francis cut off her long hair. Clare exchanged her elegant dress for a habit made of heavy cloth, with a piece of rope for a belt.

"Here is your sister! Here is Lady Poverty!" Francis exclaimed.

Peace and joy!

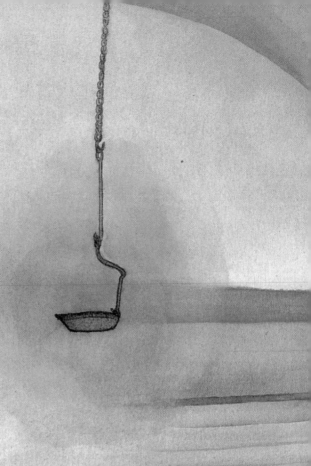

Francis led Clare to San Damiano. Her younger sister soon came to join her. Their uncle was very angry but he knew that nothing could make them change their minds. The Lord soon sent them other sisters. Together the little group prayed, loved and served God. The sisters believed and lived what Francis told them, "Perfect joy lies in being poor in everything." They called themselves the Poor Ladies of Assisi.

One winter in the countryside around Assisi...

A thick layer of snow covered the ground. Francis was called by the people of Gubbio, a town terrorized by a wolf. The starving wolf was attacking everything that came near it, sheep, children and poor beggars.

Francis went out to meet the wolf. He made the sign of cross over it.

"Brother Wolf, come here. I have something to tell you."

The wolf obeyed. It came up to Francis and placed its paw in his hand.

"I want you to be at peace with the people," Francis said gently.

"But I'm terribly hungry," replied the wolf.

"Brother Wolf, if you behave differently, you'll have a happy life in this town," Francis promised.

So the wolf stopped its attacks and from that day on it was fed by the people of Gubbio.

After the winter was over, Francis set out again. Even though he was ill, he decided to go and fast and pray for forty days on Mount Alverne, just as Jesus had done in the desert. Three of his brothers went with him. Francis was very weak. He had to ride their donkey.

But he continued to be amazed at God's creation. "How beautiful nature is!" he cried.
"Look at those hills! Those cypress trees! Those fields of beautiful green grass!"

When the little group reached the mountain they were surrounded by a flock of birds. This filled Francis with joy.

"I see that our Lord Jesus is pleased that we're going to live here for a while," he said. "I'll stay in that cave, Brother Leo."

"Our brothers the birds are celebrating," Brother Leo pointed out.

"Yes," agreed Francis, "they're singing with us. Praise and bless my Lord. Give him thanks and serve him with great humility."

On the night of September 14, 1224, Francis was praying in his cave. "Lord Jesus, I would like to love like you. You loved us by suffering on the cross."

In the morning Brother Leo met Francis. "You've been wounded, Francis!" he exclaimed. "You have wounds like Jesus on the cross!"

"Please don't tell anyone, Brother Leo," Francis pleaded.

Francis and his brothers went down into the valley again. Francis wanted to keep on preaching, but he was too weak. He went back to live near the little chapel of St. Mary of the Angels, where he had begun his life for God.

Francis was now very ill. He called Brother Angelo and Brother Leo. He asked them to sing the prayer he had written, his Canticle of Brother Sun. At the end, Francis added a few new words, "Praised be you, my Lord for our Sister Death..."

Francis was getting ready to go to heaven. He had one of the brothers read this piece from the Gospel, "Jesus knew that the hour had come for him to pass from this world to the Father. Having loved those who were his own in the world, he loved them to the end."

After sunset on October 3, 1226, a group of little birds began to circle above Francis's room. Inside he lay naked on the bare ground. While his brothers were singing a psalm, Francis peacefully closed his eyes and went home to the God he had loved so much.

Peace and joy!

A few words to help you better understand St. Francis's life...

Canticle of Brother Sun

Francis wrote this poem, which is also a prayer of praise to God, in 1225 in the little church of San Damiano. It was the first great poem which was not written in the Latin language. Francis wrote it in Italian.

Crusade

In the Middle Ages (the years from about 500 A.D. - 1450 A.D.) a crusade was a war which was considered "holy". Crusades were led to defend Christianity. At the time Francis lived there were many crusades, like the one led to free the tomb of Jesus, which had been taken by the Turks when they moved into Jerusalem.

Fast

To fast means to go without food. By giving up eating for a short time, a person offers God a sacrifice and shows that he or she depends only on God.

Gospel

This word means "good news". The good news

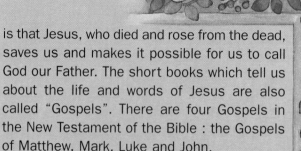

is that Jesus, who died and rose from the dead, saves us and makes it possible for us to call God our Father. The short books which tell us about the life and words of Jesus are also called "Gospels". There are four Gospels in the New Testament of the Bible : the Gospels of Matthew, Mark, Luke and John.

Peace and joy
This was the message of Francis to the world - to live in the peace and joy that the Gospel brings. Francis always greeted people by saying, "May the Lord give you peace !" Francis was filled with the peace and joy he found when he chose to live a poor life as Jesus had done.

Preaching
Preaching means announcing and explaining something. In many sermons Francis announced and explained the good news of the Gospel.

Psalm
The psalms are prayers and songs found in the Old Testament of the Bible. We can use them to pray on our own or with others. The psalms help us to talk to God about things that make us happy or sad. They help us praise God for the wonderful things he has done.

Some interesting facts about St. Francis...

In his own Italian language Francis was called the "Poverello". This means "the little poor one." Francis was able to give up money and the many nice things he liked so that he could be free to concentrate on loving God and other people. Being poor and free was so important to him that he used to say that he had married "Lady Poverty." The vow of poverty is one of the three vows or promises to God that are made by men and women in the religious life.

Because St. Francis begged for his food and the things he needed, he was called a mendicant friar ("friar" means "brother"). St. Dominic lived in France, at the same time that St. Francis lived in Italy. Like Francis, he traveled all over the country preaching the Gospel of Jesus. He was a mendicant friar too, and begged for what he needed. According to legend, St. Dominic

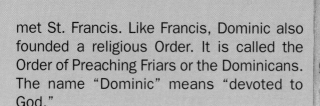

met St. Francis. Like Francis, Dominic also founded a religious Order. It is called the Order of Preaching Friars or the Dominicans. The name "Dominic" means "devoted to God."

On November 29, 1223, Pope Honorius III approved the official Rule of the Order of Franciscans founded by Francis.

In December 1223, St. Francis celebrated Christmas with the townspeople of Greccio. He was a deacon and he sang the Gospel in his gentle voice. Many people came to the Christmas Mass. Francis set up the first nativity scene or Christmas crib for the occasion. He wanted to help the people to picture what the birth of Jesus in Bethlehem had been like. The scene included a stable, a donkey, an ox and a baby wrapped in swaddling clothes, lying in a manger filled with straw. Today we still follow the custom of setting up nativity scenes at Christmas.

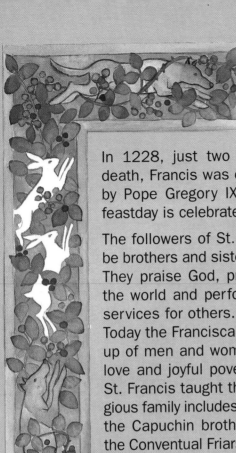

In 1228, just two years after his death, Francis was declared a saint by Pope Gregory IX. St. Francis's feastday is celebrated on October 4.

The followers of St. Francis want to be brothers and sisters to all people. They praise God, pray for peace in the world and perform many loving services for others.

Today the Franciscan family is made up of men and women who live the love and joyful poverty of Jesus as St. Francis taught them to. This religious family includes the Friars Minor, the Capuchin brothers and sisters, the Conventual Friars Minor, the Poor Clares founded by St. Clare and reformed by St. Colette, many other congregations of sisters and the Secular Franciscan Order.

Prayer

(Based on the Canticle of Brother Sun by
St. Francis of Assisi)

All-powerful and good Lord,
may everyone and everything you have made
praise and honor you.

We praise you, Lord,
with all your creatures,
especially with our Brother Sun
who gives us the day
by which you light our way.
Brother Sun is beautiful and bright.
He is a symbol of you, Lord.

We praise you, Lord,
for our Sister Moon and for the Stars.
You created them
and put them in the sky for us.

We praise you, Lord,
for Brother Wind,
and for the air, the clouds
and all kinds of weather.

We praise you, Lord,
for Sister Water.
She is so useful and humble and good.

We praise you, Lord,
for Brother Fire.
Through him you light up the night.

We praise you, Lord,
for our sister, Mother Earth.
She carries us and feeds us
with all sorts of good food.
She gives us flowers of a thousand colors
and green grass and trees.

We praise you, Lord,
for those who forgive
others out of love for you.
You will reward them in heaven.

We praise you, Lord,
for our Sister Death,
who takes our
bodies back to you.

We thank and praise you, Lord,
for everything! Amen.

 *BOOKS & MEDIA*

CALIFORNIA
> 3908 Sepulveda Blvd., Culver City, CA 90230; 310-397-8676
> 5845 Balboa Ave., San Diego, CA 9211; 619-565-9181
> 45 Geary Street, San Francisco, CA 94108; 415-781-5180

FLORIDA
> 145 S.W. 107th Ave., Miami, FL 33174; 305-559-6715

HAWAII
> 1143 Bishop Street, Honolulu, HI 96813; 808-521-2731

ILLINOIS
> 172 North Michigan Ave., Chicago, IL 60601; 312-346-4228

LOUISIANA
> 4403 Veterans Memorial Blvd., Metairie, LA 70006; 504-887-7631

MASSACHUSETTS
> 50 St. Paul's Ave., Jamaica Plain, Boston, MA 02130; 617-522-8911
> Rte. 1, 885 Providence Hwy., Dedham, MA 02026; 781-326-5385

MISSOURI
> 9804 Watson Rd., St. Louis, MO 63126; 314-965-3512

NEW JERSEY
> 561 U.S. Route 1, Wick Plaza, Edison, NJ 08817; 732-572-1200

NEW YORK
> 150 East 52nd Street, New York, NY 10022; 212-754-1110
> 78 Fort Place, Staten Island, NY 10301; 718-447-5071

OHIO
> 2105 Ontario Street, Cleveland, OH 44115; 216-621-9427

PENNSYLVANIA
> 9171-A Roosevelt Blvd., Philadelphia, PA 19114; 215-676-9494

SOUTH CAROLINA
> 243 King Street, Charleston, SC 29401; 803-577-0175

TENNESSEE
> 4811 Poplar Ave., Memphis, TN 38117; 901-761-2987

TEXAS
> 114 Main Plaza, San Antonio, TX 78205; 210-224-8101

VIRGINIA
> 1025 King Street, Alexandria, VA 22314; 703-549-3806

CANADA
> 3022 Dufferin Street, Toronto, Ontario, Canada M6B 3T5; 416-781-9131
> 1155 Yonge Street, Toronto, Ontario, Canada M4T 1W2; 416-934-3440